Fortune Cookie Wisdom

Words to Live By

By: **G. Jimmy Rheinhart Jr.**
Photo By: **G. Jimmy Rheinhart Jr.**

Fortune Cookie Wisdom

Words to Live By

By: **G. Jimmy Rheinhart Jr.**
Photo By;   **G. Jimmy Rheinhart Jr.**

Introduction

It has taken me and my family, almost thirty years to gather all the fortunes for this book. Let me explain; we saved most of the fortunes inside the fortune cookies we get with our Chinese food. Most of us have had Chinese food, whether it be delivery, take-out, or dine-in. At the end of that meal, we will read the fortunes and try to make them fit our lives or our hopes for the future. Some of us assign a meaning or some aspect of our lives we want that fortune to be about. Things like finding love, a soulmate, a job, money, vacations, and just about everything in between. I guess we're all looking for good news or an uplifting message to help get us thru our daily lives.

Once we've read and discussed the fortunes, we place them in a jar.   Once that jar gets full, we move them to a decorative cookie tin, and start filling the jar again.   Of course over the years, we would get duplicates, but we would keep them anyway.

The first fortune on page 95, is one I relate to very well.   I was offered the opportunity to go on a 5 month sailing voyage from Virginia, to the Eastern Caribbean chain of islands, and back.   I said, **"YES"** of course.   I see myself in the first fortune on page 50 as well.

I hope you find words of wisdom, in this book.

*Do not follow where the path may lead.
Go where there is no path...and leave a trail.*

*No problem can stand the assault of
sustained thinking.*

*First, learn to "Give," and then the
universe will reward you.*

Courage is grace under pressure.

Only the educated are free.

Knowledge is priceless.

A big fortune will descend upon you this year.

Do not fear failure.

Little brooks make great rivers.

Bide your time, for success is near.

*Make all you can, save all you can, **give** all you can.*

Great ambitions make great men.

Mistakes show us what we need to learn.

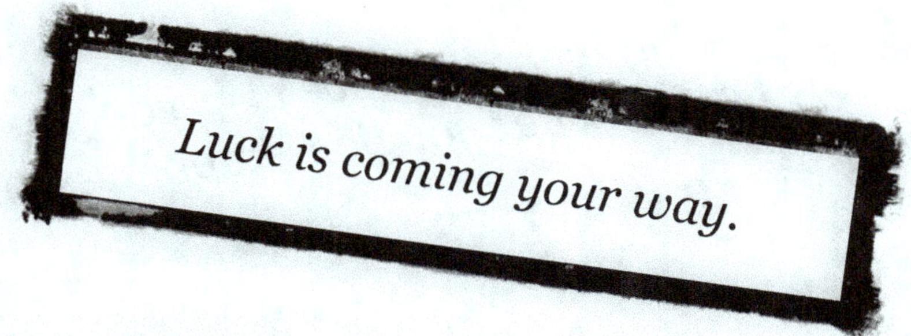

*Prepare for an exciting trip soon
to come your way.*

Today is a good day for being with a companion.

You are contemplative and analytical by nature.

A modest man never talks of himself.

*Doing what you love is freedom.
Loving what you do is happiness.*

*Enhance your karma by engaging in
various charitable activities.*

Avert misunderstanding by calm,
poise and balance.

You are a bundle of energy, always on the go.

Your home is a pleasant place
from which you draw happiness.

Wisdom is only found in truth.

The purpose of life is to live a life of purpose.

Getting the right answers is only possible when you have asked the right questions.

Every person is the architect of his own fortune.

A thrilling time is in your immediate future.

Your work interests can capture the highest status or prestige.

*You find beauty in ordinary things -
do not lose this ability.*

Face facts with dignity.

A thrilling time is in your immediate future.

Good sense is the master of human life.

The will of the people is the best law.

You will attract cultured and artistic people to your home.

You are busy but you are happy.

You could prosper in the field of medical research.

You are heading for a land of sunshine. You will always have good luck in your personal affairs.

You never hesitate to handle the most difficult problems.

*Birds are entangled by their feet
and men by their tongues.*

A happy event will take place shortly in your home.

You will pass a difficult test that will make you happier.

An empty stomach is not a good political advisor.

*You are careful and systematic in your
business arrangements.*

> *You are generous to an extreme and always think of the other fellow.*

Well-arranged time is the surest sign of a well-arranged mind.

You are going to have some new clothes.

Your home is a pleasant place from which you draw happiness.

You will take a chance on something in the near future.

You are a person of culture.

You will have many friends when you need them.

You are never selfish with your advise or your help.

You are provided with the material things you need.

You have an ambitious nature and may make a name for yourself.

You will step on the soil of many countries.

It is better to have a hen tomorrow
than an egg today.

You could prosper in the field of engineering.

You love a challenge.

The culture and customs of China attract you.

If your desires are not extravagant
they will be granted.

Your courage will bring you honor.

Try it, you may like it.

Winners expect to win in advance.
Life is a self-fulfilling prophesy.

It tastes sweet.

Speak only well of people and you will never need to whisper.

There are riches headed your way.

Your work interests can capture the highest status or prestige.

You like participating in competitive sports

You will always be surrounded by true friends.

You lead a useful life no matter what
riches are coming to you.

The night life is for you.

Time is money.

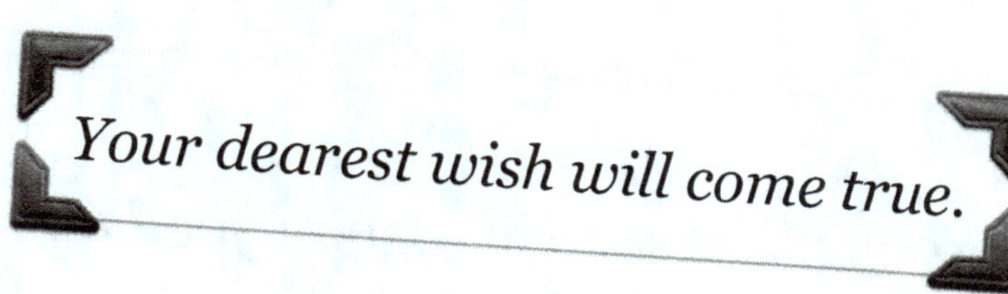

Your dearest wish will come true.

Stop searching forever,
happiness is just next to you.

Struggle as hard as you can for whatever you believe in.

You are loyal to your family.

Your lost item will be found next week.

You will be showered with good fortune.

You are a person with a strong sense of duty.

You have an active mind and a keen imagination.

The first blow does not fell the tree.

A golden egg of opportunity falls into your lap this month.

You have a deep appreciation of the arts and music.

Every man is a volume if you know how to read him.

You display the wonderful traits of charm and courtesy.

Believe in miracles.

Happy news is on its way to you.

The smart thing is to prepare for the unexpected.

Time to tie up those loose ends into beautiful bows.

You are not afraid of storms, for you are learning to sail your ship.

The possibility of a career change is near.

A billionaire's joke is always funny.

You will be successful in love.

You will make a name for yourself.

A calm sea does not make a skilled sailor.

You have only begun to scratch the surface of your real potential.

Ignorance on fire is better than knowledge on ice.

Correction does much, but encouragement everything.

All things in moderation — even moderation.

A different world cannot be built by indifferent people.

Your mind is original, creative, and alert.

Real is all a vision.
You have to see it for yourself.

You are working hard.

This is a time for love and affection.

Meeting adversity well is the source of your strength.

Courtesy is contagious.

Your dream will come true, when you least expect it.

Angels are among us; when you find them, cherish their presence everyday.

Your smile brings happiness to everyone you meet.

Deep faith eliminates fear.

An agreeable romance might begin to take on the appearance.

Follow your instincts when making decisions.

It's fun being a kid.

Accident is the mother of invention.

You are generous to an extreme
and always think of the other fellow.

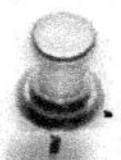

Versatility is one of your outstanding traits.

The worst bankruptcy in the world is the person who has lost his enthusiasm.

You will travel far and wide,
for both pleasure and business.

One of the keys to happiness,
is a bad memory.

*Think like a man of action,
act like a man of thought.*

*Don't be afraid to smile, you never know
who's falling in love with it.*

Don't build your happiness on other's sorrows.

Courtesy pays.

Aspire to be great — Then help others.

You will move to a wonderful new home
within the year.

If we do not change our direction, we are
likely to end up where we are headed.

If you are wise with your decisions,
good things are bound to come.

Make all you can, Save all you can,
Give all you can.

Your winsome smile will be your sure protection.

*The life of every woman or man —
the heart of it is pure and holy joy.*

*The intention is not to see through people,
but rather to see people through.*

Happiness depends upon ourselves.

*Your love of life will be happy
and harmonious.*

Your future is as boundless as the lofty heaven.

Good health will be yours for a long time.

Passionate new romance appears in your life when you least expect it.

Learn from how people in the arts react to criticism.

Laziness is nothing more than the habit of resting before you get tired.

A merry heart does good like a medicine.

Good luck bestows upon you.
You will get what your heart desires.

Don't spend your time stringing and tuning your instrument. Start making music now !

Be tactful: do not overlook your own opportunity.

There will be plenty of time to work hard; enjoy yourself !

Give yourself a day off — at least give yourself a relaxing evening.

You won't be bored for long! New adventures are on their way.

The healthy and strong individual is the one who asks for help when he needs it.

Your kindness is surely to be repaid.

You have a chance to help someone out right now in a big way.

Soon, someone will make you very proud.

Careful thinking will command respect.

Your fortune is not something to find,
but to unfold.

Good things will come to you in due course of time.

*A phone call to a good friend will ease
your mind and lift your spirits.*

*The only thing we know for sure about future
developthents is that they will develop.*

Efficiency is doing better what is already being done.

Maxim for life: You get treated in life the way you teach people to treat you.

A lifetime friend shall soon be made.

Practice random kindness and senseless acts of beauty.

Happiness isn't in having what you want but rather in wanting what you have.

Our life is the creation of our mind.

Feeding a cow with roses does not get extra appreciation.

To effect the quality of the day is no small achievement.

Your existence has a positive contribution to mankind.

Instead of worrying and agonizing, move ahead constructively.

You are talented in many ways.

Fate happens now, you decide.

Catch on fire with enthusiasm and people will come for miles to watch you burn.

Good things are being said about you.

Begin nothing until you have considered how it is to be finished.

He who laughs, lasts.

Where there is ambition, there is success.

You will be surrounded by luxury.

Today it's up to you to create the peacefulness you long for.

Your talents will be recognized and suitably rewarded.

Punctuality is the politeness of kings and the duty of gentle people everywhere.

There is a gradual improvement. Feelings are sweet and tender.

You are a perfectionist. Don't spoil it.

Nothing gets in the way of your vision of yourself in the future.

Good news will come to you by mail.

The greatest patience is humility.

Your ability to help others may not be seen by all.

God will give you everything that you want.

Love mankind, trust the majority,
and never owe anyone.

A smile is the most effective medicine

You will become more and more wealthy.

Good things are coming to you
in due course of time.

The thought that leads to no action is not
thought — it is dreaming.

Get to the point and keep it clear and simple.

Face facts with dignity.

If we are all worms, try to be a glow worm.

We learn by practice.

No one grows old by living,
only by losing interest in living.

Accept no other definition of your life,
accept only your own.

Adapt to circumstances
in order to make progress.

Your mind can make your body rich.

An hour with one friend is worth
more than ten with strangers.

Your present plans are going to succeed.

Everyone agrees you are the best.

> <u>*Softening your attitude opens your heart.*</u>

Happy event will take place shortly in your home.

Open up your mind. Let your fantasies unwind.

It is not the outside riches but the inside ones that produce happiness.

You take an optimistic view of life.

You value freedom — grant it to others.

The essential condition of everything you do must be choice, love, and passion.

You will enjoy doing something adventurous this weekend.

<u>An unexpected event will bring you riches.</u>

Great men live dangerously, small men don't take chances.

Success is never final and failure never fatal. It's courage that counts.

A clean tie attracts the soup of the day.

Desire, like the atom, is explosive with creative force.

This is a good time to consider formally helping others.

Absence, makes the heart grow fonder, makes the paycheck go lighter.

Your exotic ideas lead you to many exciting, new adventures.

Your luck will completely change today.

You may be hungry soon; order a takeout now.

Go confidently in the direction of your dreams.

True worth is in being, not seeming.

You have a yearning for perfection.

Your future is as boundless as the lofty heaven.

He who expects no gratitude shall never be disappointed.

A family reunion in the coming months will be tremendous success!

It takes courage to grow up and turn out to be who you really are.

*Relations are like investments.
The more you put in, the greater your return.*

We are very happy together.

*Experience is what you get when
you don't get what you want.*

*If you don't have time to live your life now,
when will you?*

*Today, you are wiser than usual,
and also less anxious.*

Work hard and you will become more wealthy.

You cannot make two people like each other.

A day without smiling is a day wasted.

The Master doesn't take sides; same as your spouse.

You are going to have a very comfortable old age.

Nothing can keep you from reaching your goals.

The time is right to make new friends.

Your dearest wish will come true.

The only sure thing about luck is that it will change.

Don't get so caught up in the daily grind that you never find and time to enjoy yourself.

Stop waiting! Buy that ticket, take that special trip!

When the flowers bloom so will great joy in your life.

Today is probably a huge improvement over yesterday.

Opportunities surround you if you know where to look.

Good luck is the result of good planning.

A big fortune will descend upon you this year.

Be a generous friend and a fair enemy.

*You have great physical powers and
an iron constitution.*

A short vacation is in order for you.

I have a dream...Time to go to bed.

The kind of advice we do not like to take often turns out to be the best.

You are going to take a trip to the seaside.

A kind word will keep someone warm for years.

There is someone owing so many thanks to you.

Only the person who risks is truly free.

Don't stop dreaming, otherwise sleep will get awfully boring.

Your life is like a kaleidoscope.

Politeness costs nothing and gains everything.

No job is so simple that it cannot be done wrong.

It is not only important to add years to your life, but to add life to your years.

You are headed for a land of sunshine.

Look up an old friend if you are feeling down.

You will be showered with good fortune.

He who seeks will find.

Love yourself first and everything falls into line.

Never quit!

To be content with little is true happiness.

Water not only can keep a ship afloat, but also can sink it.

Go for it. You never know whom you might run into.

Discipline is the refining fire by which talent becomes ability.

*Make your life an exclamation,
not an explanation.*

He who hurries cannot walk with dignity.

Live in **THIS** moment.

Chance favors those in motion.

*To see an old friend is as agreeable
as a good meal.*

> **Simplicity is the ultimate sophistication.**

You will be singled out for promotion.

It is very possible that you will achieve greatness in your lifetime.

A thrilling time is in store for you.

You will find great contentment in your daily routine activities.

Of all the things you wear, your expression is the most important.

No bird soars too high if he soars with his own wings.

*Look around;
happiness is trying to catch you.*

You always know the right times to be assertive or to simply wait.

Lucky you; Get out your party clothes.

Education is the ability to meet life's situations.

To affect the quality of the day is no small achievement.

We are what we think

In life, it's good not to get too comfortable.

Sorrow of parting will bring happiness of reunification.

The other line always moves faster.

You have an unusually magnetic
personality.

Failing to plan is planning to fail.

If the table moves, move with it.

Don't repay a kindness, pass it on.

There is no mistake so great as that of being always right.

You have had a good start. Work harder!

You cannot love life until you live the life you love.

Versatility is one of your outstanding traits.

Soon, your old friends will remind you of your forgotten childhood joys.

Human Rights:
Know them, Demand them, Defend them.

You are a lover of words.
Someday you should write a book.

It's not the years in your life, but the
life in your years that count.

Happy life is just in front of you

**An unexpected relationship will
become permanent.**

We can admire all we see,
but we can only pick one.

Today, put away the diplomat in order
to protect your own interests.

Open up your mind.
Let your fantasies unwind.

A journey must begin with a single step.

Imagination is everything.
It is the preview of life's coming attractions.

You will have a long life and eat many **fortune cookies**.

<u>A dream you have will come true.</u>

You will always get what you want through your charm and personality.

There are no bad days;
Some are just better than others.

Your business will assume vast proportions.

Your deeds today will be your memories tomorrow.

Share your joys and sorrows with your family.

Today's a day to nourish yourself. Feed yourself well.

You have tasted the bitterness as well as the sweetness of coffee.

<u>Have a beautiful day.</u>

*Life is not a problem to be solved
but rather a mystery to be lived.*

*Success is when you get what you want.
Happiness is when you want what you get.*

*Yet mystery and reality emerge from the
same source.*

Wisdom is the principal thing.

*You love sports, horses and gambling
but not to excess.*

*You have a potential urge and
the ability for accomplishment.*

You are going on well with your business.

Loser's visualize the penalties of failure.
Winners visualize the rewards of success.

*Discontent is the first step in the
progress of a man or a nation.*

When things go wrong, don't go with them.

You shall soon make a long, overdue
personal decision.

The only way to catch tiger cubs
is to go into the tiger's den.

Good fortune is always on your side.

You cannot be anything
if you want to be everything.

If your cookie is in two pieces, the answer is yes.

<u>*Your intelligence is something to be admired.*</u>

Your luck has been completely changed today.

*If you have a job without aggravations,
you don't have a job.*

Happiness is activity.

*Don't be afraid of opposition;
Remember a kite rises against the wind.*

The less one has to do,
the less time one finds to do it in.

Inch by inch life's a cinch.
Yard by yard life is hard.

Be adventuresome, try a new look.

Attitude is more important than facts.

Recognition is the greatest motivator.

Imagination is everything.
It is the preview of life's coming attractions.

*Q. What is K.M.S.? A. **K**eep **M**outh **S**hut,*
the golden rule.

Sometimes travel to new places
leads to great transformation.

Even as the cell is the unit of the organic
body, so the family is the unit of society.

<u>Life is a Verb.</u>

Beware of little expenses.
Small leaks will sink great ships.

A romantic evening awaits you tonight.

Don't put off till tomorrow what can be
enjoyed today.

You are one of the people who
"goes places in life".

Faith is personal, but never private.

You will receive some high prize or award.

**Joy shared is doubled.
Sorrow shared is halved.**

Keep true to the dreams of your youth.

Those who walk in other's tracks
leave no footprints.

A danger foreseen is half avoided.

*The secret of vast riches
begins with a single penny.*

You will travel to many places.

*Be magnanimous, be trustful,
be hopeful and be patient.*

**The philosophy of one century is the
common sense of the next.**

*In prosperity, our friends know us;
in adversity, we know our friends.*

The secret of staying young is good health and lying about your age.

Advice given to you will be well worth following.

You love challenge.

It is what you haven't done that will torment you.

A truly great person never puts away the simplicity of a child.

Education is the movement from darkness to light.

Your passions sweep you away.

This instant is the only time there is.

What is the speed of dark?

You are busy but you are happy.

You have a great ability to make new friends.

Make big plans.

Do not be afraid of competition.

Come back later...I am sleeping.

You are not a person who can be ignored.

Any rough times are behind you.

Energy is equal to desire and purpose.

<u>*Never doubt logical things.*</u>

*Allow your confidence to
carry you through each day.*

A diet is a selection of food that makes someone rich.

*You can't choose how you will die,
but you can choose how you will live.*

Where your treasure is, there is your heart.

**Your mentality is alert,
practical and analytical.**

*There is nothing that costs so little nor goes
so far as courtesy.*

*Your ability for accomplishment will be
followed by success.*

You deserve to have a good time after a hard day's work.

Every artist was first an amateur.

Executive ability is prominent in your make up.

Money speaks a language everyone understands.

You will have good luck in spring.

Prosperity is in your fortune

One can never consent to creep
when one feels an impulse to soar.

If you want to win anything-a race, your self,
your life-you have to go a little berserk

It is better to ask some questions,
than to have all the answers.

You are full of hopes about your future.

*There is in the worst of fortunes,
the best chance of a happy ending.*

Our truest life is when we are in our dreams
awake.

Romance moves you in a new direction.

Do not step on anyone on the way to the top

Ask a friend to join you on your next voyage.

Wrinkles should merely indicate where smiles have been.

Versatility is one of your outstanding traits.

You will become a great philanthropist in your later years.

You will be attracted to an older, more experienced person.

You begin to appreciate how important it is to share your personal beliefs.

*Seek first to understand and then
to be understood.*

You are the guiding star of his existence.

The harder the fall, the higher the bounce.

*Win as if you were used to it,
lose as if you enjoyed it for a change.*

*You may be conservative, cautious and
practical.*

Life is not a matter of holding good cards, but sometimes playing a poor hand well.

Apply your imagination to any problem that arises.

You will do better in real estate than in stocks.

You have an iron will, which helps you succeed in everything.

Keep a cool head and bide your time; a chance is bound to come.

To see an old friend is as agreeable as a good meal.

You have a natural grace and great consideration for others.

Today brings out the performer and humanitarian in you.

You are filled up with a sense of urgency. Be patient or you may end up confused.

Persistence and determination alone are omnipotent.

Humor is an affirmation of dignity.

Believe in miracles.

Your patience has the ability to test even the sands of time.

A beautiful person is with you, confide your problems.

Opportunities multiply as they are seized, they die when neglected.

The man on the top of the mountain did not fall there.

The one waiting for you when you get home will be your friend for life

You are going on well with your business.

Simplicity of character is the natural result of profound thought.

Courtesy is one of the best peacemakers.

An angry man opens his mouth
and shuts his eyes.

A new friend will soon enter your life
with blessings to share.

*Today it is up to you to create the
peacefulness you long for.*

*You will come to realizations in
your life that change you forever.*

You are offered the dream of a lifetime;
<u>Say yes!</u>

If you don't enjoy what you have,
How could you be happier with more?

You'll never know what you can do until you try.

Good thoughts come from the heart.

Everything must have a beginning.

All happiness is in the mind.

Your talents will be recognized and suitably rewarded.

A pleasant experience is ahead; don't pass it by.

Only you can change your life. No one can do it for you.

Before you roar, please take a deep breath.

Your dream life is rich — listen to your dreams.

You can fix it with a little extra energy and a positive attitude.

An empty stomach is not a good political advisor.

Ambition knows no obstacles.

You will have good luck and overcome many hardships.

Your good deeds are never forgotten.

You will be of good comfort.

One who does nothing but wait for his ship to come in has already missed the boat.

One should count each day a separate life.

Without knowing the force of words, it is impossible to know men.

There are many ways you can be hurtful, but only one way to heal. That is through love.

Seize every second of your life and savor it.

It takes more than a good memory to have good memories.

One person with a belief is equal to force of ninety-nine who have only interest.

Music is the divine way to tell beautiful, poetic things to the heart.

Have patience — it will benefit you.

Only one who attempts the absurd can achieve the impossible.

You can make a new start this week. Work hard and be diligent.

Next week, your luck color will be Green!

Telling someone the truth is a loving act.

Heroism is endurance for one moment more.

<u>Every good friend once was a stranger.</u>

*Happiness is enjoying what you got.
Never from what you want.*

*Make two grins grow where there was only
a grouch before.*

To be upset over what you don't have,
is to waste what you do have.

It can't rain all the time.

You are kind-hearted and hospitable,
cheerful and well-liked.

Let your hook be always cast. In the pool
where you least expect it, will be fish.

If I bring forth what is inside me,
what I bring forth will save me.

Inspiration within is waiting for you.
It's time to go deep.

You are a person of culture. Cultivate it.

Some say faith is nowhere.
Others say faith is now here.

May your faith always exceed your fears -
no price is too great to go through life afraid.

Attitudes are the forerunners of conditions.

Vary your friendships.

Give assistance, not advice, in a crisis.

In life, you won't go far unless you know where the goalposts are.

Find release from your cares, have a good time.

A house without books is like a room without windows.

You should let go of negative things today.

Every friend takes joy in your success.

You have a secret admirer.

The greatest ownership is embracement of emptiness.

Efforts and courage are not enough without purpose and direction.

The strangest, most generous, and proudest of all virtues is...True Courage.

You can't have everything...
where would you put it all.

You are alert to the events and feelings around you.

Buy things because you need them,
not because they are on sale.

If the brain were so simple we could understand it,
we would be so simple we couldn't.

It's time for you to explore all those new interests.

When you gather all your resources together, goals are accomplished.

It only gets better when **YOU** get better.

How many of you believe in psychokinesis? Raise my hand.

You will step on the soil of many countries.

*Generosity will repay itself
sooner than you imagine.*

Good sense is the master of human life.

A closed mind is like a closed book;
Just like a block of wood.

Working hard will make you have a happy life.

Suppose you can get what you want....

*Opportunities surround you,
if you know where to look.*

A new business venture is on the horizon.

The star of riches is shining upon you.

Listen to everyone.
Ideas come from everywhere.

Success is in starting a new project at work.

The only thing worse than being talked about is not getting talked about.

Look ahead or you won't get ahead.

It is necessary; Therefore, it is possible.

Listen to life, and you will hear the voice of life crying; Be!

You will enjoy good health.

Faithless is he who quits when the road darkens.

It is up to you to create your own adventures today!

To make dreams real, first you have to have them.

Don't build your happiness on other's sorrow.

Learning is a treasure which accompanies us everywhere.

Acting on a good idea is better than just having a good idea.

You are smart, for you do things smartly.

Don't just spend time; invest it.

You never hesitate to tackle the most difficult problems.

You will soon discover how truly fortunate you really are.

Our first and last love is . . . self-love.

<u>*You are never bitter, deceptive, or petty.*</u>

You like participating in competitive sports.

Nature, time and patience are the three great physicians.

On the right track, means need to run even faster, or get run over.

You will soon take a very pleasant and successful trip.

Your next business venture will be very profitable.

When the moment comes, take the last one from the left.

You will spend old age in comfort and material wealth.

The secret of success is constancy of purpose.

Winners expect to win in advance.
Life is a self-fulfilling prophesy.

You will be successful in your work.

To build a better world, start in your community.

A wise man knows everything, a shrewd one knows everyone.

Believe it can be done.

Expect much of yourself and little of others.

*If you have knowledge,
let others light their candles by it.*

*If you don't think about the future,
you can't have one*

*If you wish to see the best in others,
show the best of yourself.*

*Be tactful; do not overlook your own
opportunity.*

Many people who have power
become a deaf-mute.

Some people like to give advise,
but not listen to their own.

Character development is the true aim of education.

Only you can change your life.
No one can do it for you.

Conscience is a man's compass.

Don't scrap everything!
See what you can salvage.

I hear and I forget. I see and I remember.
I do and I understand.

A cheerful letter or message is on its way to you.

Advise comes in all forms;
some help you and some hurt you.

When you feel like quitting —
Think about why you started.

If it is meant to be, who are you to change that. Time to believe it.

A person's character is his destiny.

Soon you will be sitting on top of the world.

Our truest life is when we are in our dreams **awake.**

The small steps you take will ultimately bring you great fortune.

Pleasant experiences make life delightful.
Painful experiences lead to growth.

The true sign of intelligence is not knowledge, but imagination.

Next time, order the shrimp.

Study metaphysics — you will find much to appreciate.

Service is the rent we pay for the privilege of living on this planet.

Good work, good life, good love, good-bye oppression.

Impossible standards just make life difficult.

If you want to succeed in business, avoid "Business as usual."

He who believes is strong; he who doubts is weak.

*If you want to add value to your life,
take care of every moment.*

Utility is when you have plumbing,
luxury is when you have a pool.

<u>*Whatever you do, do it with all your heart.*</u>

*Well, why not? Admit it —
you're intrigued.*

There are plenty of promises and
hope floating around you.

This is the month that ingenuity stands high on the list.

Truth, can you handle the truth?

There is no rose without a thorn.

*There is but one cause of human failure.
And that is man's lack of faith in his true self.*

<u>*There is no time like the pleasant.*</u>

*Though I am not naturally honest,
I am so sometimes by chance.*

*Time is nature's way of keeping everything
from happening all at once.*

Tomorrow is a new day;
You should begin it well and serenely.

Try a new system or different approach.

Time is the wisest counselor.

Those who do not remember the past
are condemned to repeat it.

To affirm is to make firm.

*To be able to look back upon one's past life
with satisfaction is to live twice.*

You are what you think about all day long.

Turn on the charm. You'll be glad you did.

*To give anything less than your best
is to sacrifice the gift.*

*You must be willing to act today
in order to succeed.*

Think highly of yourself, for the world takes you at your own estimate.

Age can never hope to win you while your heart is young.

A beautiful person is with you, confide your problems.

Your simple kindness today will be rewarded multiple times.

Beauty is in the mirror you look at everyday. Enjoy your being.

He who enjoys doing and enjoys what he has done is happy.

Everything is perfect in the universe - even your desire to improve it.

Enthusiasm is the greatest asset in the world. It beats money, power, and influence.

True love is only found in the heart.

There's more to balance than not falling over.

*To avoid criticism, do nothing, say nothing,
be nothing.*

What makes an apple fall to the ground?

*To think is easy; to act is difficult.
To act as one thinks is the most difficult of all.*

*Today is probably a huge improvement
over yesterday.*

*This is not a day to take risks.
Diplomacy rules today.*

To give happiness is to deserve happiness.

Where there is ambition, there is success.

You or a close friend will be married soon.

A smooth long journey! Great expectations!

You cannot be anything
if you want to be everything.

Ulcers are what you got for forgetting
your stomach.

*Today's a day to nourish yourself. Feed
yourself well.*

There's no point to being grown up
if you can't be childish sometimes.

*To love and be loved is like feeling the sun
from both sides.*

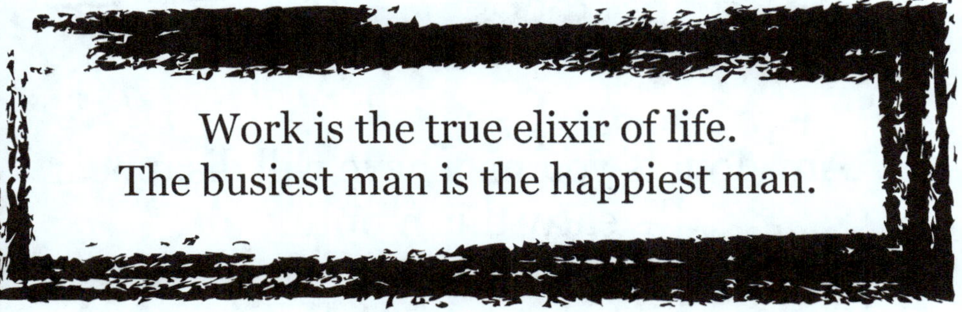

There's no problem that cannot be solved over a green tea ice-cream.

To be a success in business, be daring, be first, be different.

Think of what you will think of 10 years from now.

You are born with grace and beauty.

Any doubts you may have will disappear early this month.

You have a pair of shining eyes.

You are careful and systematic in your business arrangements.

Get ready to become the star.

You can't help everyone.
But everyone can help someone.

To get respect from others, one must give respect to others.

You can fix it with a little extra energy and a positive attitude.

You will bring sunshine into someone's life.

You will learn the value of a kind word.

Act as if it were impossible to fail.

Action is worry's worst enemy.

> *What we acquire without sweat,
> we give away without regret.*

*If you want to win anything-a race, your self,
your life-you have to go a little berserk.*

*One's mind, once stretched by a new idea,
never regains its original dimensions.*

Money will come to you when you are
doing the right thing.

Wedding bells are in a close friend's future.

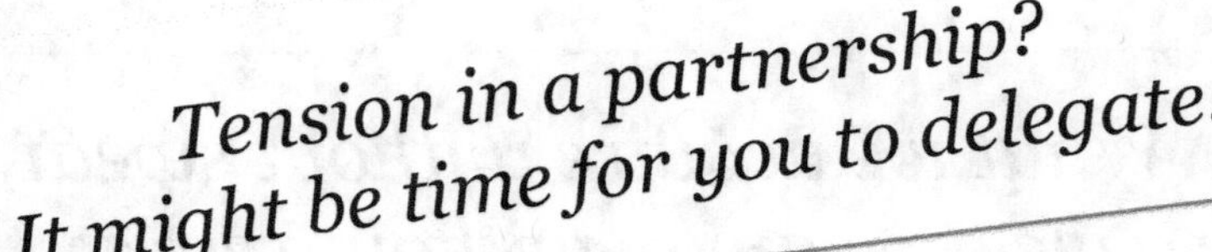

Tension in a partnership?
It might be time for you to delegate.

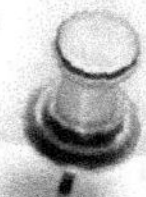

The usefulness of a cup is in its emptiness.

The current year will bring you happiness.

There is nothing lost or wasted in this life.

One old friend is better than two new ones.

*Be tactful; you will save someone
from heartache by doing so.*

Take advantage of the dynamic energy
to better your relationship.

Your smile shines in a crowd.

Your mentality is alert, practical and analytical.

You will soon be the guest of a person you admire.

Drastic means are not as necessary as you think.

Seek friendships and you will find someone special this month.

Respond intelligently even to unintelligent treatment.

The three basic ingredients of the capitalistic system: money, energy, and ideas.

Do not let great ambitions overshadow small success.

The deepest waters make the least noise.

An upcoming event will reunite you with old friends.

Take calculated risks. That is quite different from being rash.

The eye of the master will do more work than both his hands.

Maturity: Do you duty without being supervised.

You will attend an event and meet someone you admire.

The time is <u>always</u> right to do what is right.

Mend the first brake, kill the first snake, and conquer everything you undertake.

Today you are wiser than usual, and also less anxious.

Don't be afraid to take that big step.

Your hard work will soon pay off.

A short saying oft contains much wisdom.

You are a source of wisdom and
strength to many people.

A much needed vacation
will allow you to unwind.

The smart thing to do is to start trusting your intuition.

Your investments of time now will lead to success later.

Need some adventure and enjoyment? Take a vacation.

Make serious decisions in the last few days of the month.

Including others in your life will bring you great happiness.

It may be; Those who do most, Dream most.

An important discussion involving you will take place today.

Take the time to do it right , otherwise you will have to take the time to do it over.

A lifetime of happiness lies ahead of you.

The quality, not the longevity, of one's life is what is important.

It's always worth taking the trouble to
praise people.

Opportunity is knocking at your front door.
Answer it!

In the end all things will be known.

You will be graced by the presence
of a loved one soon.

You will travel to exotic places on your next trip.

<u>In order to take, one must first Give.</u>

*It's not just what you know but what you
USE of what you know that counts.*

Cooperation will work better.

*Regenerate your system through diet and
exercise. Save the cookies!*

You will enjoy good health.

*Opportunities multiply as they are seized,
they die when neglected.*

*Sitting towards the East may bring you
good fortune.*

Investment opportunities are rising.

*Look for the dream that keeps coming back.
It is your destiny.*

You will soon be surrounded by good friends.

Luck will visit you on the next new moon.

You will be rewarded for your kindness to others.

Your personality is fueled by the
fascination you feel for life.

You will attend an event and
meet someone you admire.

Romance comes to life this year
in a very unusual sort of way.

A romantic mystery will soon add
interest to your life.

You will do well in the field of
computer technology.

Tomorrow will be a productive day.
Don't oversleep.

Soon, someone will make you very proud.

The project you have in mind
will soon gain momentum.

*The strengths in your character
will bring you serenity.*

Things are not always what they seem.
It's not that bad!

*Share your fortune with others.
It will bring you good luck.*

*Remember three months from this date.
Good things are in store for you.*

Use your talents.
That's what they are intended for.

You constantly struggle for self improvement — and it shows.

The evening promises romantic interests.

You should be able to undertake and complete anything you desire.

Take no risks with your reputation.

You have an active mind and a keen imagination.

*Speak less of your plans-
you will get more of them done.*

You will bring sunshine into someone's life.

Your short term goal will soon be realized.

**Prepare for an exciting trip
soon to come your way.**

Life is a series of choices.
Today yours are good ones.

You will enjoy doing something
adventurous this coming weekend.

You will have many friends when you need them.

You will be enjoying a relaxing spa day next week.

You deserve to have a good time after a hard day's work.

**If you're not living on the edge,
you're taking up too much room.**

I ended with a saying I use a lot to get my friends to try new things in life. We hope you found this book fun and entertaining. If you came across some words of wisdom or a profound fortune you really enjoyed, try incorporating it into your daily life.

G. Jimmy Rheinhart Jr.